AMERICA'S GREATEST TEAMS

THE PHILADELPHIA PHILLIES

Sloan MacRae

PowerKiDS press.
New York

Published in 2012 by The Rosen Publishing Group, Inc.
29 East 21st Street, New York, NY 10010

First Edition

Editor: Amelie von Zumbusch
Book Design: Greg Tucker
Layout Design: Ashley Drago

Photo Credits: Cover (background) Rob Tringali/Sportschrome/Getty Images; cover (Chase Utley) Jim Luzzi/Getty Images; cover (Ryan Howard), pp. 5, 22 (bottom right) Ezra Shaw/Getty Images; cover (Steve Carlton), p. 17 Ronald C. Modra/Sports Imagery/Getty Images; p. 7 Chris McGrath/Getty Images; p. 9 Hunter Martin/Getty Images; pp. 11, 22 (top) Mark Rucker/Transcendental Graphics/Getty Images; p. 13 Rogers Photo Archive/Getty Images; p. 15 Ralph Morse/Time & Life Pictures/Getty Images; pp. 19, 22 (bottom left) Elsa/Getty Images; p. 21 Rich Pilling/MLB Photos via Getty Images; p. 22 (middle) MLB Photos via Getty Images.

Library of Congress Cataloging-in-Publication Data

MacRae, Sloan.
The Philadelphia Phillies / by Sloan MacRae. — 1st ed.
p. cm. — (America's greatest teams)
Includes index.
ISBN 978-1-4488-5008-2 (library binding) — ISBN 978-1-4488-5149-2 (pbk.) —
ISBN 978-1-4488-5150-8 (6-pack)
1. Philadelphia Phillies (Baseball team)—History—Juvenile literature. I. Title.
GV875.P45M33 2012
796.357'6409 74811—dc22
2011000155

Manufactured in the United States of America

CPSIA Compliance Information: Batch #WS11PK: For Further Information contact Rosen Publishing, New York, New York at 1-800-237-9932

CONTENTS

AMERICA'S ONE-TOWN TEAM 4
RED, WHITE, AND BLUE 6
THE PHILLIE PHANATIC 8
PHILADELPHIA QUAKERS 10
EARLY SUCCESS 12
THE WHIZ KIDS 14
WORTH THE WAIT 16
BACK ON TOP 18
HERE TO STAY 20
PHILADELPHIA PHILLIES TIMELINE 22
GLOSSARY 23
INDEX 24
WEB SITES 24

AMERICA'S ONE-TOWN TEAM

Many American sports teams have moved to different cities over the years. This may happen because a team is having trouble selling tickets. There might be a bigger team in the same city. Some teams have changed cities and names several times. The Philadelphia Phillies are special because they have not. The Phillies have played under the same name in the same city longer than any team in all of American sports!

There have been a lot of ups and downs in the Phillies' rich history. The team played through long **losing streaks**. Great players helped the Phillies turn these streaks around and win **pennants**.

Ryan Howard joined the Phillies in 2004 and quickly became one of the team's biggest stars. In 2006, he was named the National League's most valuable player, or MVP.

RED, WHITE, AND BLUE

The Phillies play in Philadelphia, Pennsylvania. Baseball fans often call the team the Phils for short. Philadelphia is one of the most important cities in American history. Benjamin Franklin, the famous American thinker, lived there. It is where the **Declaration of Independence** was signed. Philadelphia is also home to the historic **Liberty Bell**. One of the Phillies' **logos** shows the Liberty Bell and the team's name on top of a baseball diamond. Another logo is the letter *P*.

To honor their city's place in history, the Phillies wear the colors red, white, and blue. These are the colors of the American flag.

This young Phillies fan is getting ready for a game by having his face painted with the team's colors. He is dressed in the team's colors, too.

THE PHILLIE PHANATIC

The Phillies play in a **stadium** called Citizens Bank Park. Millions of Phillies fans pack the ballpark each season. Phillies fans mean business. Other teams hate playing in Citizens Bank Park because Phils fans love to make fun of them. These fans are known to be one of the loudest and wildest groups in American sports. This helps the Phillies because their fans might cause players from other teams to make mistakes or play poorly.

The Phillies have a famous **mascot** called the Phillie Phanatic. It is a furry green monster with a big, funny-looking nose. The Phillie Phanatic gets the fans at Citizens Bank Park ready for the game.

The Phillie Phanatic often rides around on an ATV, as seen here. It is 6 feet 6 inches (2 m) tall and first appeared in 1978.

PHILADELPHIA QUAKERS

The team we know today as the Phillies was formed in 1883. At that time, they were called the Philadelphia Quakers. The Quakers were a peaceful group of people who were among the first European settlers of Pennsylvania. The team's name did not stick, though. The team soon became known as the Philadelphias. Fans began to call them the Phillies for short. They have been the Phillies ever since.

Phillies fans learned early that it would take patience to root for their team. They had some good seasons, but the Phillies would not win a pennant for over 30 years.

This picture shows some of the members of the 1886 Philadelphia Phillies team. Charlie Ferguson is on the left, while Cannonball Titcomb is standing.

EARLY SUCCESS

It took a great **pitcher** named Grover Cleveland Alexander to help the Phillies become great. Alexander joined the team in 1911. Soon, the Phillies became one of the best teams in baseball. The Phillies won the pennant in 1915 and faced the Boston Red Sox in the **World Series**. This is baseball's **championship**. World Series games are the most important baseball games of the year. The Phillies won the first game, but they lost the next four. Boston won the championship.

Things went badly for the Phillies after losing the World Series. They had only one winning season between 1918 and 1948.

Even during their losing streak, the Phillies had some great players, such as Chuck Klein. He hit four home runs in one game on July 10, 1936.

THE WHIZ KIDS

The Phillies' long years of losing came to an end thanks to the Whiz Kids. These were a group of good, young players led by pitcher Robin Roberts. The Whiz Kids got the Phillies back to the World Series in 1950. This was the first time Philadelphia had reached the **postseason** since 1915. The Phils lost the World Series to the New York Yankees. However, they were once again one of the best teams in baseball.

Over the next few years, the Phillies had great players such as Dick Allen. It would take many more seasons to reach the World Series again, though.

These players are members of the great 1950 Phillies team. They include several Whiz Kids, such as center fielder Richie Ashburn, bottom row second from left.

WORTH THE WAIT

The Phillies finally won it all for their fans in 1980. The team had been on the rise in recent years. Star pitcher Steve Carlton and the great hitter Mike Schmidt led the team to another World Series. This time the Phils faced the Kansas City Royals, and they won.

The Phillies were on top of the baseball world. Players such as Garry Maddox, Lenny Dykstra, and Curt Schilling would keep them there for years to come. The Phillies reached the World Series again in 1983 and 1993. The team did not win either time. The Phillies had come a long way, though. After all, many teams never even get the chance to play in a championship.

Steve Carlton was one of the best pitchers of his time. He won four Cy Young Awards for his pitching. Carlton was called Lefty because he pitched left-handed.

BACK ON TOP

The Phillies struggled a bit after they lost the World Series in 1993. It did not take them long to get better, though. Jimmy Rollins, Chase Utley, and Ryan Howard became the stars of the 2000s.

The Phillies reached the postseason in 2007, but they fell short of getting to the World Series. The Phils were better the very next year. The great pitcher Cole Hamels led Philadelphia to its first World Series since 1993. The Phillies beat the Tampa Bay Rays to win their second championship for the city of Philadelphia. They reached the World Series again in 2009 but did not win this time.

Here, members of the Phillies celebrate their win in the 2008 World Series. The Phillies won four games in the series, while the Rays won one.

HERE TO STAY

Few teams have had as many ups and downs as the Philadelphia Phillies. They are one of the best teams in the history of baseball. Some years, though, they have been among the sport's worst teams. In fact, the Phillies have lost more games than any other **major-league** team. This is only because they have been around for so long!

The Phillies' years of losing are behind them. They have some of the best pitchers in baseball, such as Roy Halladay and Cliff Lee. No team looks forward to playing the Phillies. This is not just because of the fans. The players are also hard to beat.

Jimmy Rollins started playing for the Phillies in 2000. He quickly became a star. Rollins sometimes goes by his nickname, J-Roll. He plays shortstop.

PHILADELPHIA PHILLIES TIMELINE

1883

The Phillies play their first game. They lose to the Providence Grays.

1885

Charlie Ferguson throws the first no-hitter in Phillies history. This means no one on the other team got a hit.

1915

The Phillies lose their first World Series to the Boston Red Sox.

1950

The Whiz Kids lose the World Series to the New York Yankees.

1972

Mike Schmidt plays his first game for the Phillies.

1980

The Phillies win their first World Series.

2008

The Phillies win their second World Series.

2009

The Phillies trade Cliff Lee to the Seattle Mariners. The team would make a deal to bring Lee back the next year.

2010

Roy Halladay throws a perfect game. This means no one from the other team reached first base.

GLOSSARY

CHAMPIONSHIP (CHAM-pee-un-ship) A contest held to determine the best, or the winner.

DECLARATION OF INDEPENDENCE (deh-kluh-RAY-shun UV in-duh-PEN-dints) An official announcement adopted on July 4, 1776, in which American colonists stated they were free of British rule.

LIBERTY BELL (LIH-ber-tee BEL) A bell that came to stand for the United States' struggle for freedom.

LOGOS (LOH-gohz) Pictures, words, or letters that stand for a team or company.

LOSING STREAKS (LOO-zing STREEKS) Long periods during which a team loses lots of the games it plays.

MAJOR-LEAGUE (MAY-jur-leeg) A group of baseball teams made up of the best players.

MASCOT (MAS-kot) A person, an animal, or an object that stands for a group of people.

PENNANTS (PEH-nunts) League championship wins.

PITCHER (PIH-cher) A player who throws the ball for people to hit in baseball.

POSTSEASON (pohst-SEE-zun) Games played after the regular season.

STADIUM (STAY-dee-um) A place where sports are played.

WORLD SERIES (WURLD SEER-eez) A group of games in which the two best baseball teams play against each other.

INDEX

C
championship, 12, 16, 18
cities, 4, 6, 18

F
fans, 6, 8, 10, 16, 20
Franklin, Benjamin, 6

G
game(s), 8, 12, 20, 22

H
history, 4, 6, 20, 22
home, 6

L
Liberty Bell, 6
logo(s), 6

M
mascot, 8

N
name(s), 4, 6, 10

P
pennant(s), 4, 10, 12
Philadelphia, Pennsylvania, 6, 18
pitcher(s), 12, 14, 16, 18, 20
players, 4, 8, 14, 16, 20
postseason, 14, 18

S
season(s), 8, 10, 12, 14
sports, 4, 8
stadium, 8

T
tickets, 4
trouble, 4

W
World Series, 12, 14, 16, 18, 22

WEB SITES

Due to the changing nature of Internet links, PowerKids Press has developed an online list of Web sites related to the subject of this book. This site is updated regularly. Please use this link to access the list:
www.powerkidslinks.com/agt/phillies/